Dr. Jennifer Gilbert

Help!

Help! My Students are Bored and So Am I!

The Interactive Classroom Environment

HELP! MY STUDENTS ARE BORED AND SO AM I!
THE INTERACTIVE CLASSROOM ENVIRONMENT

iUniverse books may be ordered through booksellers or by contacting:

iUniverse
1663 Liberty Drive
Bloomington, IN 47403
www.iuniverse.com
1-800-Authors (1-800-288-4677)

ISBN: 978-1-5320-2462-7 (sc)
ISBN: 978-1-5320-2461-0 (e)

Library of Congress Control Number: 2017910139

Print information available on the last page.

iUniverse rev. date: 7/28/2017

Endorsements from my Classrooms

My favorite activity in Dr. Gilbert's room is make them majesty because make them majesty is a helping activity and I like helping. It is one of my most favorite things to do in this world when I'm bored.

My favorite activity in Dr. Gilbert's room is projects because we get to spend time with our family and we do some of it in class. One time I got to do a project about my home state of New Orleans, Louisiana.

My favorite activity in Dr. Gilbert's room is the card games because when we are in work stations you can play cards in a lot of different ways.

My favorite activity in Dr. Gilbert's room is visual aids because when I get stuck on a problem in class, I can look at it and find my answer.

My favorite activity in Dr. Gilbert's room is competitions because it makes it fun to learn. It makes you want to do more so you can win. If you win at the end, you get a prize. You are learning and having fun at the same time.

My favorite activity in Dr. Gilbert's room is make them majesty because we get to put on a crown that says we are majesty and I love it because it makes me feel like a princess.

Help!!

My Students Are Bored, and So Am I!

Also by Jennifer Gilbert

Churchin' Ain't Easy (2011)

...And Deliver Us From People! (2013)

For the Perfecting of the Saints (2014)

365 Revelatory Words for Any Given Day (2017)

Teach Me How to Live Realistically Single (2017)

The Data Driven Instructional Classroom (2017)

The Journey Back to Me (2017)

Help!!

My Students Are Bored, and So Am I!

The Interactive Classroom Environment

Dr. Jennifer Gilbert, Ed.D

This is to all of the teachers that are looking for a way to reinvigorate the manners of learning in their classroom. The ones that are ready to bring life back in to their classroom in both newer conventional and non-conventional ways.

Contents

Epigraph

There is a difference between a teacher and an educator. The teacher is in it for Summers and Christmas off, while the educator seeks to serve the whole child and thinks of their learning career, and not just the current curriculum.

"Give me a mind and I will return a miracle."

-Dr. Jennifer Gilbert

Foreword by Sherronda Randle

BRILLIANT

B= Breath taking ideas for teaching content areas.

R= Resourceful reading material for experienced teachers as well as new teachers.

I= Intriguing chapters that were intentionally put together for a successful outcome.

L= Lively material that captures the minds of all ages.

L= Lasting knowledge for all students to utilize when needed.

I= Instruction that supports a positive learning environment.

A= Activities that require students to develop their communication skills while interacting with others.

N= Nurturing material that encourages colleagues to get excited and physical about teaching.

T= Tailored for all minds to be engaged for maximum GROWTH.

This book is a book that every teacher should have as their little blue book with all the secrets in it. This book is equipped with so many comprehensible strategies that will allow students,especially ELL (English Language Learners), to develop so they can be successful in reading, writing, listening, and speaking. From chapter one all the way to chapter twenty five you will find all the activities and strategies will engage each student so they can feel they are part of a cultivating environment that allows them to move about the classroom as they learn. There are so many books out there to help teachers become effective in their delivery of knowledge to their students, but this book is a book that you can rely on time after time because the simplicity of how to use the content in each chapter. This book is a must have book, so when you buy one for yourself, buy several to give away to your teacher friends.

Preface

I chose to write this book to be used as a resource not only for new teachers, but also for the seasoned ones who realize that it is not easy teaching today's generation of learners. Gone are the days that you stand in front the class and do the normal transmission of knowledge, and now are the days that you have to nearly bring a circus act into the classroom to keep the interest while also pairing down on the students and preparing them with the stamina to sit in silence for an extended period of time and take high stakes standardized testing. This book takes all of these components into consideration.

This book is not just for the secular classroom, but can be used in any educational forum to include vacation bible schools as well as the regular Wednesday night Bible Study. Any location that you want, desire, or expect learning to take place, this book can be used. You will be surprised how much adults would appreciate the breaking of the monotony of the traditional classroom environment.

This book is dedicated to all of my fellow educators that are still trying to figure it all out. Trying to see how all of the puzzle pieces go together to create an environment that is conducive to productivity and is exciting for the students, which gives the results that administrators are looking for and makes your job a lot easier.

Introduction

When we went to college, we were prepared for pedagogy, filled with theory, and overloaded with standards and expectations. No one ever really takes you by the hand and shows you how to bring about the most important function to the students which is how to make learning fun again. Fun is the only interest that many students have in the learning process. They don't become invested in it until they see that they can enjoy themselves while working. You bring the fun and they will bring the learning. It is what I call "The Great Exchange!"

This book will give you a photograph of the concept that I speak of, the methodology behind it, the direction to facilitate it, The resources needed to create the artifact and even the educational benefits of it in case your administration asks.

This is a very easy read that is fun, educational, and entertaining.

Important Components to an Interactive Classroom Environment

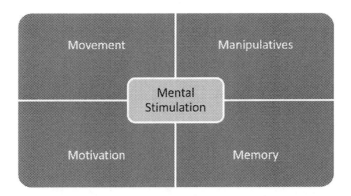

There are some important components to an interactive Classroom Environment as well as some things that have to be in place in order for the environment to be productive and successful.

The Four Building Blocks of in an Interactive Classroom Environment

The first things we need to talk about are the four building blocks of the interactive classroom environment: movement, manipulatives, motivation, and memory.

Movement-

There are six purposes of movement in the classroom which is; to prepare the brain for learning to incorporate specific brain compatible movements that can improve neural connections, to provide brain breaks which can give the brain the opportunity it needs to process and consolidate information, supporting exercise and fitness to encourage healthy living, to develop cohesion through movement activities can prepare the brain for learning new information, reviewing content through movement during the lesson is the ideal way to use repetition to improve retention, and lastly teaching content through movement which will help many students of all ages and cultures understand and retain information. This is the short version of the purposes.

There are a number of studies that show favor towards movement in the classroom and the effects that it has on the brain. Without getting too scientific and to keep this as simple as possible, I encourage you to think about the different hats that you, as an adult, wears in life. For example, I am a mom, a grandma, an educator, a singer, a minister and of course an author. When I operate in these different roles, I act differently because there is a different element of my being that is called forth as I move from one position to the other. For instance, it is very difficult for me to write in my bedroom because it disrupts my personal rest and my professional flow. As I move into my home office, I can push out the pages, but I cannot get comfortable to rest. So it is in the classroom. When students move from one place to another and transition from one activity to another, their mindsets change. Though nothing has changed but their position and the expectation, the students nearly always sit down in their new station or in their new activity and say, "Okay, now...." It is so interesting to watch. Try it in your room and see how they act, and the first words out of their mouth when they begin a new activity.

Manipulatives

Using manipulatives is a great way to get students engaged in the learning process. The manipulative business is the largest income generator in the education field because they too are based on scientific findings that manipulatives are not only good for kinesthetic learners, but it also plays a part in the lives of all students and the retention of information that was transmitted. No matter the learning style, when one is able to encounter the information by doing it, hands on, then they are much more likely to remember it.

Motivation

The interactive classroom is all about motivating the student to learn the material that is being taught in the classroom. Motivation is defines as the disposition of learners that is characterized by their willingness to initiate learning activities and continued involvement in a learning task and their long term commitment to learning. There are two types of motivation; intrinsic and extrinsic. Intrinsic motivation is when the learner does the task for internal reasons such as pleasure or enjoyment in the activity. Extrinsic motivation is where the students come to complete the task for external reasons such as to please a parent or to avoid getting into trouble with the teacher. Most students always start off learning for extrinsic reasons, but the idea of the interactive classroom environment is to get them to transcend over from extrinsic to intrinsic motivation. It is all about making the learning environment fun.

Memory

Getting students to commit things to memory is all about making the activity fun and memorable. It goes back to stimulating interest. There are 6 ways of stimulating interests that serve as the foundation that this book is built on.

1. Find ways to get students actively involved in the learning process.
2. Assess students' interests, hobbies and extracurricular activities.
3. Relate content and objectives to student experiences.
4. Occasionally present information and argue positions contrary to the students' assumptions.
5. Support instruction with humor, personal experiences, incidental information, and anecdotes that represent the human characteristics of the content.
6. Use divergent questions and brainstorming activities to stimulate active involvement.

With that being said there are some things that must be set in place before fun can begin. Before we get to the fun we will explore a few housekeeping rules that must be met first, let's call them "Interactive Precautions."

Interactive Precautions

Interactive Precautions are the matters that must be established prior to the interactive learning environment implementation. These precautions are

- Classroom Management
- Rules and Procedures
- Relationship

Classroom Management

There is an art to classroom management, either you have it or you don't. It can be taught, but for the most successful it is just a trait that you possess. Classroom management is being able to control a classroom no matter the modality of learning. It is going to be very difficult to create an orderly, interactive classroom without prior classroom management. I am that one teacher that others use to threaten their students into acting orderly. No matter what grade I teach the other teachers, call Dr. Gilbert to assist with their disciplinary issues. I'm not offended; I just call it "a gift." The gift of being able to show love to the students, but also be firm and let them know that we came here to learn and not kick it and be friends. You will witness as you read this book that I am one for acronyms. My first acronym for classroom management is;

Classroom

M-Making

A-All

N-New

A-Academic

G-Gains

E-Engaging

M-Memorable

E-Enjoyable

N-Notable And

T-Testable

Classroom management is all about...

- Knowing your students
- Knowing their interest
- Knowing how to be interactive without overstimulating
- Learning how to transcend from teacher to facilitator
- Organization

Without the above components classroom management is nearly impossible.

Rules and Procedures

Rules and procedures are not just items that you run through the first day of school. It is something that you continuously practice and intentionally draw attention to everyday. Routines and procedures in the classroom is all of the stability that some students know. The more that they know about what is expected of them, the less work it takes to get things done. The rules and procedures that I am talking about here are different from the rules and procedures that I cover in the activities section of the book. You will see the difference when you get to that section. For now I am just trying to let you know how important regular routines and procedures come into play when trying to create an interactive classroom environment. They must first know what normal looks like before they can embrace the interactivity of the classroom otherwise to them the classroom becomes a circus with no sense of normalcy.

Relationship

The importance of relationship with students in an interactive environment comes into play because you have to know your students. You have to understand their personality first. Who is shy and who is more outgoing? Who are the leaders and who are the followers? Who knows the material and who just plays like they don't know the material just to be cool? Who can you trust to be the leader in the activities such as workstations or learning centers when the answers are available? Can you trust them not to cheat? These are all a part of the relationship that you build with students and then they will feel as though it is safe to get the wrong answer. This feeds back into Maslow's Hierarchy of Needs [1] that I have adopted and modified into Gilbert's Hierarchy to an Interactive Learning Environment.

---

[1] https://simplypsychology.org/maslow.html

Maslow's Graphic/ Gilbert's Hierarchy to an Interactive Learning Environment

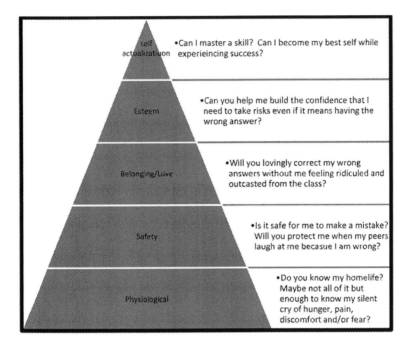

• self actualizatiuon — •Can I master a skill? Can I become my best self while experieincing success?

Esteem — •Can you help me build the confidence that I need to take risks even if it means having the wrong answer?

Belonging/Love — •Will you lovingly correct my wrong answers without me feeling ridiculed and outcasted from the class?

Safety — •Is it safe for me to make a mistake? Will you protect me when my peers laugh at me becasue I am wrong?

Physiological — •Do you know my homelife? Maybe not all of it but enough to know my silent cry of hunger, pain, discomfort and/or fear?

Activities

Now to the fun we have all been waiting for the interactive classroom environment activities. Each activity is a different chapter and follows the following format;

- **Methodology**-What this activity is all about...
- **Directions**-How to complete this activity.
- **Resources**-The resources needed for this activity either hand-made or store bought
- **Educational Benefits**-This is the part that explains the educational benefits of the activity.

Chapter One

Learning Centers with a Twist

Methodology:

Learning Centers and workstations are oftentimes used interchangeably. The reality is that they are two very different concepts especially when used correctly. The learning centers that I am speaking of in this book are all about the authenticity of learning centers. Each center is set up with a different concept. You can use data such as test scores and concepts that are historical struggles for your grade level for these learning centers. These come after you have taught the concept and have pretty much closed it out or even as a reinforcement while you are teaching that unit. As you can see in the pictures above I went and purchased a deck of cards with different reading concepts such as inferencing, cause and effect, context clues and the like. I use one deck of cards at each station accompanied with a pair of dice and a game board.

Directions:

The students roll the dice to see how many spaces they move, they read the card and choose the correct answer. If they choose the correct answer they move forward, if their answer is incorrect they move backwards. When an incorrect answer is chosen, then the group has to assist with coming up with the right answers with justifications.

Resources:

You can make cards, but it is much easier to purchase the cards from Edupress because the passages are grade level appropriate with scaffold levels of rigor. For instance this year I am teaching third grade and the cards range from grades 3.5-5. The cards have the answers on the back so that the students can get the correct answers with ease.

Educational Benefits:

Because the passages are short, the students are reading a lot more and this in turn increases fluency, exposes them to additional vocabulary. This also brings about cooperative learning and allows for the students to step up as peer tutors

Workstations versus learning center chart

Workstations	Both	Learning Centers
• Traditionally work on a single concept with multiple steps and each location is a different step or is a different element of a single step objective. For instance for the writing process, I have one station for each part of the writing process, however, for objectives like cause and effect, each station is a different story where the students have to find a number of cause and effect relationships in the passage.	• Provide a change of state. • Assist in breaking down instructional elements and objectives in different ways	• Normally works on different objectives and concepts at once in each location to reinforce skills and scaffold in different elements of instruction.

Chapter Two

Workstations

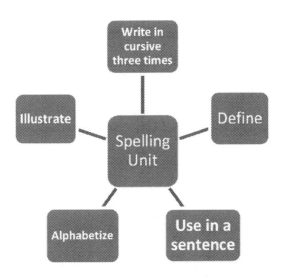

Methodology

Workstations are what most teachers use as a traditional interactive methodology for their students. Workstations can be done in so many different ways. There is really no right or wrong way to do it, you just have to do what works for you and your students. The illustration that I am using above is for a spelling unit because that is the easiest to explain the methodology. As stated in our comparison chart, workstations break down a single element or objective into parts so that the end result is the same. Each week I give my students a spelling unit and they always have objectives that they must complete in class. To ensure that I don't take up too much class time with spelling, especially during the test prep season, I place the spelling unit in workstations where the students rotate to complete different components of their unit.

Directions

The way that I facilitate my workstations is by placing the materials for each station in the middle of the table with the students. I then allot a certain amount of time in each station, normally about ten minutes. After the ten minutes the students rotate clockwise to the next station. Once they are settled I start the timer again and I continue this process until all workstations are complete. To accommodate my slower learners, once students get back to their home station, I normally give them about ten more minutes to check their work and complete any stations that they were not able to finish in the allotted time.

Resources

The resources for workstations are some sort of containers that can be used to store all materials needed for that workstation. I will either use the timer on my phone or I will put the online timer on the screen for all the students to see and gauge themselves and their progress according to the timer. (You definitely have to take into consideration the knowledge that you have of your students. For some the posted timer stresses them out, and then of course there are those who will play around until the last minute and then try to do all their work quickly and carelessly.)

Educational Benefits

This interactive activity has many educational benefits. One of the main benefits is that it is a versatile activity that breaks a concept into achievable chunks. It also brings about a change of state. When the students go from one station to another and they work on a different activity, it causes the brain to reset itself and prepare to take on a new task. The timer adds adrenaline to the tasks at hand. This modality is also good for students who suffer with different attention issues.

Chapter Three

Playing Cards

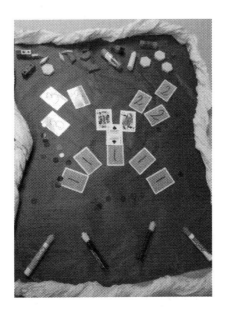

Methodology

Who would've thought that a deck of cards could and would bring so much life into a classroom? Playing cards are my biggest motivators. We all know that students love competition. With a single deck of cards, I can reward correct answers, I can give random number of points, and I can also use the cards as a grouping randomizer. Notice on the picture that I number my decks of cards so that I can know that I have a full deck if I needed to do something more structured with the cards as well.

Directions

For this section I will give directions for just a few of the ways that I use the playing cards.

- *Motivator*
  Whenever I am not getting the participation that I want from my class, my safety net is to always go get my buckets with the cards in it. When they see that, the hands go up like firecrackers. This motivates them because they know the party is about to begin in one of the ways mentioned below.

- *Competition*
  When I use the cards for competition mode, I ask a question and the students with the correct answer gets a random card. If they can justify their answer, depending on how well they do it, they can get anywhere from one to three more cards. If they work as groups, the group with the most cards wins.

- *Points*
  When I use the cards in points mode, I do one of two things, I will give them the number of points that I want them to have according to the number on the cards or I can just give them cards at random and they have to add up the value of the cards and not just the number of cards.

- *Grouping random*
  When I use it for a group randomizer, I give the students a card and then call either the suit or the number on the card and that is who is responsible for completing the task or reporting to a certain group or station.

Resources

The resources are very simple, you can just go to the dollar tree and purchase decks of cards, take a sharpie and number them, place the different decks in separate Ziploc bags. I also purchase the little plastic containers from the dollar store to stack my various manipulatives in.

Educational Benefits

Though we would love for all students to be intrinsically motivated, let's be honest, it just doesn't happen like that often. Students are fearful when it comes to schoolwork for a number of reasons. They are fearful of failing, fearful of disapproval, shy, confused or just apprehensive. For whatever the reason it is that the students won't join in on the fun, it is all alleviated when they see those cards come out. Even the shyest of students throws their hands up. They know that at the end, they have a chance for the treasure box and I keep it stocked. I play the game with the cards on the most difficult of concepts until they become confident in it and then I take the cards away to transition them from extrinsic to intrinsic motivation.

Another great reason for these cards is that it gets the students talking especially when you give them more cards for their reasons and rationales. This takes learning to a whole other level because it creates academic dialogue as does our next activity.

Chapter Four

True/ False Flags

Methodology

True/False flag are the greatest way to promote great academic conversations. I use these flags all the time because it causes the students to not only choose an answer, but justify their answer. This is the greatest level of learning to me.

Directions

There are a number of ways that you can use these items. During test prep, I choose an answer and the students have to tell me if my answer is true or false and then tell me how they know that. I also allow the students to use these flags to agree or disagree with a classmates answer as well. However you do it, the object of the game is to get them talking productively.

Resources

To make these flags, I just used craft sticks. I created text boxes on my computer and put true or false on them. I then laminated them and cut them out and finally stapled them to the craft sticks. I then purchased the containers from the dollar store to place them in when not in use.

Educational Benefits

The educational benefit as I have mentioned times before is all about creating opportunities for dialogue for them. We all know that students want to talk and be heard, this is the platform that they need to talk productively. You also get a real time opportunity to check for understanding and clear up any misconceptions in a fun, yet direct way.

Chapter Five

Yes/No Flags

Methodology

Much like the true /false flags, the yes/no flags also create an opportunity for dialogue as well. I use the yes/no flags more for processes for subjects such as math when I am asking which operation, and also what step I should do next but the big questions is mostly, "Am I done with the problem?" Question stems that are conducive to the answers yes or no naturally are what these flags are used for.

Directions

The directions for this are quite simple. You are to use these more for processes and procedures of subject matter.

Resources

To make these flags, I just used craft sticks. I created text boxes on my computer and put yes or no on them. I then laminated them and cut them out and finally staple them to the craft sticks. I then purchased the containers from the dollar store to place them in when not in use.

Educational Benefits

The educational benefit as I have mentioned times before is all about creating opportunities for dialogue for them. We all know that students want to talk and be heard, this is the platform that they need to talk productively. You also get a real time opportunity to check for understanding and clear up any misconceptions in a fun, yet direct way.

Chapter Six

Multiple Choice Pinch Cards

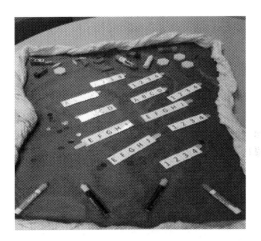

Methodology

Pinch cards are not uncommon to the interactive classroom. As you can see from the picture above, I made pinch cards for all multiple choice questions as well as writing prompt ratings of 1-4. This is where you can do a quick check for understanding on quizzes, tests and other elements.

Directions

For this activity the students would normally have a multiple choice artifact and after you read the question you ask the student to pinch their answer choice on the pinch card. You have to look quickly because if they see their answer choices are unpopular, they will look around and then change their minds. To alleviate this issue, I always read the question, have them pinch their cards to themselves, close their eyes and show at the count of three. This brings another level of excitement to the activity. I would then graph the answers and see how many chose what answer and then we would check the right answers and I would have one person from each wrong answer explain to me what they did wrong. This is another way of promoting dialogue in the learning environment.

Resources

To make these flags, I just used craft sticks. I created text boxes on my computer and put the letters or numbers on them. I then laminated them and cut them out and finally staple them to the craft sticks. I then purchased the containers from the dollar store to place them in when not in use.

Educational Benefits

The educational benefits of this activity serve as a corporate check for understanding. You can scaffold in graphing and again my favorite is that you can promote educational dialogue by allowing the students to show you what they did, not only to get the right answer, but most importantly the wrong answer. In all of these activities, I serve as only the facilitator of the action, like the director of the play. The implementation of the artifacts bring about all of the instruction and the students do all of the work, especially after you have done these activities a few times.

Chapter Seven

Competitions

Methodology

We are all fully aware of the fact that students love to compete against one another. There are so many ways that we can create good, healthy, wholesome, fun, and competitive activities, but I like to do it in my workstations with my students competing, at times, amongst themselves, within their team.

Directions

With this activity, most of the time I use the cards from learning centers with a twist. The students roll the dice; they pull a card and answer the questions. If they answer the question correctly, they move forward, if they are incorrect, they have to move backwards. If they get to the start line while moving back, then they just begin to lose a turn. The first one to the finish line wins or the one who is closest to the finish line when the timer goes off wins.

Resources

For this I just created a candy land type game board and then I laminated it. I made about ten of them so that I could have one at each workstation and also in case they get ruined in any manner. I also use dice for the students to roll and see how many places to move and of course poker chips for them to move on their spaces.

Educational Benefits

The educational benefits of this activity is that the students are fully engaged in what they are doing. This is what I call having fun with a purpose. The great thing about this is that this activity can be done in workstations with a twist over different standards and objectives using the same resources.

Chapter Eight

Routines and Procedures

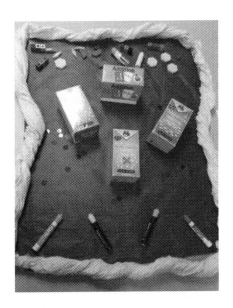

Methodology

Many people would ask why did I put routines and procedures first in this book and then again here? Well the answer is clear. Though routines and procedures definitely help with classroom management, that is not what this book is all about. Now, what I am going to talk about under this methodology is intentional learning opportunities that are often overlooked such as transition times like bathroom and water breaks, while waiting in line at lunch, while waiting for buses during dismissal and any other downtimes that you may find throughout the days that are consistent.

Directions

- Restroom breaks
- Water breaks
- Lunch lines
- General assembly in the morning or dismissal
- Warmups

During the above mentioned times are what I call intentional learning opportunities. It is times that you must have throughout the day each day, but you are losing structured class time. This is the time where you can go over math facts using the cards as shown in the picture. It is also a time that you can go over spelling words, quiz over components such as parts of speech and other like objectives that the students need to remember, you can even have book chats. Of course it should be done quietly as to not disturb other classes, but you also don't want to lose a minute of learning. I have found the most successful to be spelling reviews and math facts. These are things that you don't really want to lose instructional time going over every day, but it is something that needs to be covered repeatedly.

Resources

The resources would vary according to whatever it is that you are reviewing. Again I have found flashcards and spelling lists to be the best because one person can be showing them while the others are taking turns going to the restroom or getting water or whatever the case may be. (NOTE: It has also been my experience that when you do this activity students move quicker to go the restroom and get water and get back in line so that they can participate in the game.)

Educational Benefits

The educational benefits of this is that it speeds up their math fact fluency, it also alleviates most undesirable behavior that usually transpire during downtimes such as the ones described.

Chapter Nine

Dominos

Methodology

Who would've thought that a simple set of dominoes could be so beneficial in the learning environment? Okay, I admit, I am in Dollar Tree shopping recovery. It is a place that I go in to sharpen my ability to think outside of the box for my classroom. I look at all of their artifacts and I think of what could I use this for and how else can I use that? Dominoes are something that my family plays often when we come together. However, dominoes also have great educational value in the math department. I use it in so many ways.

Directions

- ***Fractions creation***
  With this activity I have the students to draw the fraction that the domino that they pull says.

- ***Create equivalent fractions***
  With this activity, the students pull a domino and then they have to create an equivalent fraction to go with the domino.

- ***Comparing Fractions***
  With this activity, the students pull two dominos and they compare the fractions and say whether the first is greater than, less than or equal to the second one.

- ***Addition fluency***
  With this activity, the students add the two numbers on the dominos and they race to see who can get the most dominoes right in one minute.

- ***Multiplication fluency***
  With this activity, the students multiply the two numbers on the dominos and they race to see who can get the most dominoes right in one minute.

- ***Subtraction fluency***
  With this activity, the students subtract the two numbers on the dominos and they race to see who can get the most dominoes right in one minute.

Resources

Several sets of dominos

Educational Benefits

This is a fun way of doing math and the numbers are random and cannot be manipulated. There are a number of other ways that you can use dominos just like with the decks of cards. Have fun and let your imagination run wild.

Chapter Ten

Interactive Word Walls

Methodology

There are so many forms of word walls. Some are store bought like the ones I took pictures of above; there are others that are handwritten. There are some made up of themes like the ones above and others are just from spelling tests and units of instruction. Many educators use word walls in different ways, and the ways you can use them are endless. I am going to name just a few ways to use them interactively where they are placed and used intentionally.

Directions

- ***Scavenger hunt***

The students will go to the word wall and look for words that fall under certain characteristics like syllabication, cvc [2], vccv [3], stable syllable [4], r-controlled [5] and many other ways that you can group words. This can be done at random and actually turned into a workstation.

- ***Sentence Creation***

Students can go to the wall and use a prescribed number of words to create sentences using the various sentence types.

- ***Handwriting***

The students can use the word wall to practice writing words in cursive or in print.

- ***Today I learned...***

As the days go by and students are writing, the students learn how to spell new words. Students can be chosen at random to go and put a word on the word wall that they learned that day so that others may see and know how to spell that word correctly as well.

Resources

I personally like using the store bought word units because they are more colorful and decorative. The words are also grouped accordingly as well. I also use the today I learned but the students

---

[2] http://infomory.com/what-is/what-are-cvc-words/
[3] http://fultonpds.pbworks.com/w/page/48636318/CVC,%20CVCe,%20CVVC%20Patterns
[4] http://www.readingrockets.org/article/six-syllable-types
[5] http://www.phonicsontheweb.com/r-vowels.php

place it on their personal word wall in their journals which is the next activity that we will talk about.

Educational Benefits

This activity of course increases the students' vocabulary, which will in turn affect their reading fluency. The more words that they know it also assists them in their writing efforts and decreases the likelihood that they will have repetitive words in their writing.

Chapter Eleven

Journaling

Methodology

Journaling is another method that falls under so many categories of learning. One way is that it is an organizational technique. It is also evidence of consistency, structure, and organization. As you can see from the pictures of my own classroom, I have journals for writing and for reading. For math, they call their journals scratch pads, but it is the same concept. For their reading journals, I use a program called Target Reading and it has a separate set of instructions than my writing and interactive journals.

Directions

- ***Reading-***
  As I stated for reading I purchased a program called Target Reading. I have grade levels 3, 4 and 5. I currently teach

third grade, but I use all 3 grades to increase rigor as the year progresses. What I do is I tape up the 5 questions that go with the passage. The students get 10 minutes to write down the questions in their journal headed with the title of the passage and the date. When they are done, they go to the carpet and read the passage silently. When the timer goes off the entire class meets at the carpet and we read the story together. I then ask them my personal daily 5 questions which are the 5 components of instruction that is found in every story because students normally struggle with them and that is inferencing, text structure, author's purpose, sequencing and genre. When I am done there and we have analyzed the text, the students go back to their seats and answer their questions in 10 minutes and then we go over them and they get a grade. This is what my reading block looks like daily and it's done first thing in the morning. It is a part of our routine so the students already know exactly what to do.

- *Writing*
  No matter the grade the students get a writing prompt once a week and the students record the prompt and the date in their journals and then they complete their writing. I then check their journals and give them a score from 1-4 which equates to 25, 50, 75, or 100 and again this is kept in the classroom over the course of the year.

- **Interactive Journal**
  The interactive journal is where we keep all of the foldables that we create throughout the year. We make the foldables freehand and then we glue them into our interactive journals and the students use their interactive journals as a resource when we move on to other concepts.

- **Scratchpads**
  The students call their journals scratch pads for math because this is where they actually show their work for their math problems that we do together in class.

Resources

Notice that I use the composition books for journals. This is because I cannot take the pieces of paper that fall all over the place when the students use spirals. I also like the neatness and permanence that comes with using the composition books. You can use either one, but my preference is the composition books.

Educational Benefits

There are sooooo many educational benefits for this and many documentation purposes can be served through this methodology for the teacher as well. One of the educational benefits is that if you start journaling in the beginning of the year, the students can see their own progress over time. It will also serve as documentation for special populations and can be used in ARD meetings and other special meetings as well. Whether students do the work or not these can be used for documentation for parents, administrators, and special interest individuals.

Chapter Twelve

Acronyms

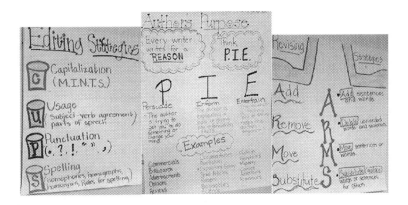

Methodology

So you think it is strange that I would put acronyms in an interactive classroom environment book? When you see how I use them you will understand why. Acronyms are sayings that are associated with a concept to help students remember and apply the concept to their practice and application using a skill. For instance, when students are learning capitalization I use the acronym of M.I.N.T.S. for the main components that you should capitalize.

M-Months

I-The letter I

N-Names of Proper Nouns

T-Titles of People and Books

S-The start of a sentence

Directions

There are so many uses for acronyms. I use them as chants and turn them into cheers and songs in my classroom. I also give them to the gym teacher and let him use them to countdown exercise activities. You can also use them as a reminder when reading over their writing journals. You can just put the acronym and make the students do a scavenger hunt for the corrections that they need to make.

Resources

I always use chart paper as you see pictured above to make my anchor charts and of course sharpies. I am not the best artist so I use Pinterest for a lot of ideas and then I also allow my students to draw the latest cartoon characters on it and then that gives them vested interest in the concept because they see their work publicized. I also allow the students to draw the anchor charts in their interactive journals as well.

Educational Benefits

The educational benefits of using acronyms are that the brain can better memorize the concept. It segments and organizes the information in a way that enables a higher capability to recall the information.

Chapter Thirteen

Learning Themes

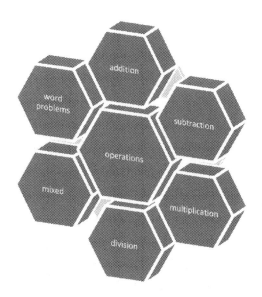

Methodology

The learning themes that I am speaking of are not the typical cutesy learning themes where you have a theme like animals and all of your instruction revolves around that. I am talking more of the content learning themes where if you are able to create your own scope and sequence for your classroom that you do it to where all of your components tie in together in some form. For math, it just makes sense to do things like operations. The first operation one would do is addition, then subtraction, then multiplication and lastly division. Once you are done with the operations in isolation then you want to have a week to mix them up and address key words for each as a strategy for word problems.

Directions

With this I would take a week for each operation and then a week of mixtures and then of course a week to address word problems and keywords. This teaching in isolation first allows you to see which operation each student is deficient in and therefore you will know what you need to work on and also what operation to tell the parents to assist with. Another measure that I track during this time is the students' fluency for math problems.

Resources

There are a number of websites and methods to completing this assessment and I usually check the student fluency once a month to ensure that the students are getting faster with their math facts.

Educational Benefits

Creating learning themes allows students to make connections amongst concepts easier and it flows better for you as the teacher. I used math for an example, but you can also do the same for all subjects.

Chapter Fourteen

Stop Light Learning

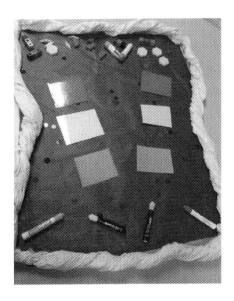

Methodology

This is a great way to check for understanding. This is a nonintrusive way of doing that. There are always those students that are ashamed of showing that they don't understand something which speaks to the truth that you, as the facilitator have to make the environment safe for correction. This is one way of doing this. The students can show their stop light that is used according to their understanding and you know where to stand or with which group to spend more time with.

41

Directions

As you are teaching, you can have the students to hold up the stop light that depicts their understanding of the concept. You, as the facilitator, can stop at regular intervals and ask, "How are we?" When you ask that question that is a cue for the students to hold up their stop lights. Red is for "I'm lost", Yellow is for "I'm not sure" and green is for "We are good."

Resources

For this artifact, I just took card stock and laminated it and cut it into fourths. This is a very simple artifact to make. You could also add what each color means to the card if you like, but we use this so much in my class the students just know what they mean.

Educational Benefits

The educational benefit to this is that the facilitator can do a consistent check for understanding during the interim of teaching. This way you don't have to wait until the end of the lesson to see if they got it. Many times it's just one component of the objective that they struggle with. This lets you know exactly where they are lost. This is also a gauge for you, as the educator, as to whether you are going too fast or not.

Chapter Fifteen

Visual Aids

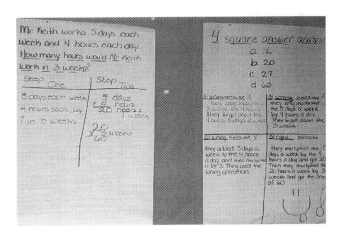

Methodology

Visual aids come in many forms such as anchor charts, bulletin boards, foldables and much more. Visual aids serve as a resource to the objective at hand.

Directions

As you prepare to teach each concept, ask yourself which visual aid modality would be best and then you can research to see what visuals others have used and either adopt those or tweak them and make your own visual aids.

Resources

Resources for visual aid assistance are plentiful. Google images are always great. My coworkers and I are avid fans of Pinterest as well. I usually start with visual aids like anchor charts and then I also create a foldable or another resource.

Educational Benefits

The benefits of visual aids is that it assists all learners, especially English Language Learners. It also serves as a resource throughout the year. A common practice for me is that I allow the students to copy my anchor charts inside of their interactive journal for later use long after I have taken the anchor chart down. The interesting thing is that this method also engrains it in their head because they were able to draw it.

Chapter Sixteen

Make them Royalty

(King and Queen of...)

Methodology

The methodology behind this interactive activity is clear, to groom students to become future leaders. No matter the grade or the age people want to be looked up to. Why not market on that momentum and make it official. This activity boosts the confidence of the struggling and motivates and occupies the ones who have already mastered the skill. This also frees the teacher up to do things such as small groups and the like.

Directions

For this activity, the class is normally working on a single skill and the masters of that skill become like the peer coaches or lil' teachers. You can call them whatever you like but also call them your life savers. You set up a station with these students where the other students can go and ask for help if needed. You can have the royalty set a timer for the time that they spend assisting a student. For the sake of structure I would set a timer for just a minute or two for assistance and then the students have to go back and finish their work. This way you can better control the atmosphere and the conversation.

Resources

For this activity you can take sentence strips and laminated sheets of paper and staple them together to make the crowns or some people go to places like McDonalds, Burger King and the like and get their little crowns and use those. You can also go to a party store or even the dollar tree. Whatever your budget, create them as you please but remember to have some way that they all stand out from the rest.

Educational Benefits

Have you ever had to reteach an objective and you had a few students who had already mastered the skill so they felt the need to entertain the class while you teach? Well this is the activity for you and for them. Turn those few into leadership and put them to work. You can turn those students into the objective wizards that can assist others while you do things like small groups and the like. This keeps them occupied, keeps the class on tasks and allows you to do other things. This actually motivates the class as a whole and it shows them how they too can one day be the wizard.

Chapter Seventeen

Think Maps

Methodology

Have you been looking for an artistic way to organize and present information that can also be an organizational tool for the thought patterns of students? Think maps is the way. There are a number of them already in existence but you can always fee freel to allow students to create their own as well.

Directions

The best way to make this work is to use the think map program as pictured above and/or other graphic organizers to include the smart art on the word program of your computer. If this is your first time using think maps and your first time introducing it to your students, I would recommend you all using the same one for your objective. I always encourage students to ensure that their information is accurate but also to be creative as well. Students start off apprehensive, but as time goes on, they become more comfortable with it and you will find them using them on everything.

Resources

There are a number of different graphic organizers that you can use. I possess a program that is actually called "Think Maps." You can also use Word and any other graphic organizers that you can find online or in any textbook.

Educational Benefits

Think maps are another sort of visual aid that assists all students especially ESL (English as a Second Language) groups and special education students. Graphic organizers helps the brain organize and process different information effectively and makes it easier for application to take place.

Chapter Eighteen

Pre and Post Postings

Pre and Post Testing Template		
Student Name	Pre Test Score	Post Test Score

Methodology

I always tell my students that the 100s that you get are small battle victories of the war that you are trying to win. Nevertheless, with that being said, I like to allow the students the opportunity to see their own growth. Pre and post testing is just one of the ways that I do that.

Directions

Pretesting is just a short quiz that I give on Mondays to see how in depth I may or may not need to go into our objective for the week or in some cases for the day. The post test is something that I do either at the end of the day, the week or the objective. I allow the students to either track it in their personal journals and/or I track it as a class and place it on the board. The objective is to see the score go up. When it doesn't, I ask the students "Are you telling me that you learned nothing?" If the scores decreased, I ask the, "Are you telling me that you forgot some of the information that you already knew?" This questioning brings this methodology home to them and helps them to make sense of the task at hand.

Resources

For this tracking, I simply use Word and make my own tracking device and each student gets their own for their data tracker and/or I create one on the data board for the classroom.

Educational Benefits

The educational benefits of this activity help the students to see how the learning process takes place. It lets them compete with themselves to get a better post test score than they did on their pretest. This allows them to keep a fresh perspective on each objective.

Chapter Nineteen

Dice

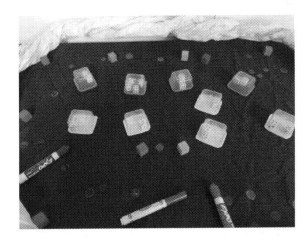

Methodology

Dice can be used in soooooo many ways inside of the classroom. Many think that you can use it only for math, but there are a number of other ways and reasons that you can use it. I am just going to tell about a few of the many ways that I use it in my classroom.

Directions

Randomizer- I use the dice to randomly choose numbers for the students to do in math. It also acts as a randomizer for the students themselves.

Place Value -The students roll the dice a certain number of times and then they record the numbers that they get and then I have the students write the words in standard form, expanded form, word form and the like.

Fact Families- Also allow the students to create fact families using the dice as well. They first start off with a yes or no as to will it work evenly and then if it is a yes, they create the family, if it is a no then they roll again.

Movement-Traditionally tells the number of places students move during games.

Resources-

You can get dice in bulk from amazon or even from the dollar tree.

Note: I also buy the little boxes from family dollar to put them in so that when they are rolling the dice, they don't fly everywhere.

Educational Benefits

The dice alone bring an element of fun to the learning experience. It is outside of the safety zone for many children. No one has any control over the numbers that are produced and therefore it keeps the students on their toes.

Chapter Twenty
Projects

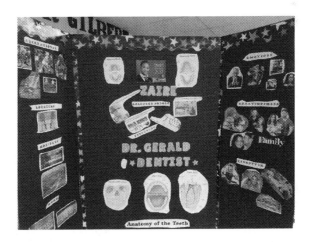

Methodology

Projects are always fun. I am not sure who enjoys them more the students or I. My normal practice is that I group together a number of standards and I create a project out of it. I normally touch all subjects with my projects and the students are expected to complete one project per grading period.

Directions

Create a rubric for your project

Make three columns as shown in the back of the book

Project Name		
Due Date		
A brief explanation of the project		
Laymen's terms objective	Standard of learning	Point value
TSWBAT (the student will be able to...)	3.22aiv	_____/10

Resources

When creating my projects, I always consult the state standards, my scope and sequence, and then I use Word to create a rubric. I usually use the same rubric for a number of years and all I have to do is change the due dates.

Educational Benefits

The educational benefits of my projects are that it fosters collaboration between home and school. It allows time for parents to assist with their child's learning process. It gives the students something to look forward to each grading period and of course, my favorite, it also adds the element of fun to learning. At times, I even add a presentation element to the assignment so that the students get used to public speaking. Projects are the greatest way to combine elements of a single unit together for a common goal.

Some projects that I have done over the years are;

- 50 state unit pt. 1- the students are given a map of the 50 states with the states printed on there and they are given a blank map. Each week for four weeks the students are given a 50 state test. The objective is that at the end of the four weeks, the students are to increase the number of states that they know. I do not take a grade each week, but of course I don't tell them that. The project grade comes at the end of the 4th week when the expectation is that they know all 50.

- 50 state unit pt. 2- the students each pick a state and then they create a brochure for their state that tells a number of elements including where the state is located on the map as well as the flag, the resources, the economy, the politics and the like. It all depends on your state standards
- Business plan-the students create their dream business and then they tell about their overhead, expenses, how to make their product, whether they would be domestic or international and many other elements.
- Regions of Texas- This is sort of a drill down from the state projects except now we explore the state of Texas. The students create a time line, the resources for each region and many other elements.

Chapter Twenty One

Foldables

Methodology

Foldables are a sort of extension to the graphic organizers and think maps that we talked about earlier. Foldables are another creative way of organizing and/or practicing a skill. They come in many forms and new forms are always being created.

Directions

I have different foldables for different skills. I normally first decide on the skill and then I peruse through my foldables and choose an appropriate one for the skill and incorporate that into my lesson.

Resources

There are a number of books that contain different types of foldables. I also consult, my favorite, Pinterest for ideas as well. You can also google ideas. All it normally takes is just paper and scissors and maybe a stapler.

Educational Benefits

The educational benefits for graphic organizers and foldables are nearly the same. They are both ways that allows one to manipulate information in many ways and to apply the information as needed.

Chapter Twenty Two
Labs

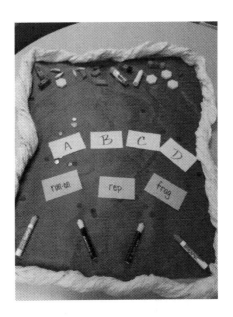

Methodology

When most people hear labs, the first thing that they think of is science. The truth of the matter is that labs can be manipulated to fit all subjects. This again makes the lesson more interactive and interesting, not to mention exciting for the students.

Directions

I create labs again depending on the content that I am trying to convey. Therefore the directions will be different for each lab. Some of the labs that I have done in days gone by are:

Contraction operation, in which the students use tweezers and scissors to cut out the part of the whole word and then stitch it back together with a Band Aid to make a new word called a contraction.

Sentence surgery, where the students dissect a sentence and remove words that should not be in sentences and place the correct words in the sentence.

Misspelling repellent- the students take misspelled words and do surgery on them to make them where they are spelled correctly.

Making a path for math- I create an esophagus for numbers and the students have to place the numbers inside the esophagus that goes with that objective. (I do this for even/odd numbers, fact families, factor trees and the like.)

Resources

The resources again depend on the type of lab that you do. My normal resources are scissors, disposable gloves, face masks that painters/surgeons use, Band-Aids, paper, scissors and preprinted materials from the objective.

Educational Benefits

This makes the lesson come alive. Doing the surgeries also help the hand-eye coordination of the students and it also is a more memorable experience because the students will have the removal of the wrong and the insertion of the right ingrained in their brains because they manipulated it themselves and the experience was fun.

Chapter Twenty Three
Task Cards

Methodology

Task cards are cards that have tasks or questions on them for the students to do independently or in a collaborative group. You can make or buy them and they can be used as a form of assessment or in conjunction with workstations and other independent modalities.

Directions

The directions come from the task cards themselves. The ways that you use them can be manipulated, but the cards usually stay the same.

Resources

I have found task cards on Teachers Pay Teachers, Pinterest, and I have also created them from prior state exams as well as other mediums that I have ran across.

Educational Benefits

Task cards have a number of benefits. They promote collaboration when used in group settings; they can be used as a check for understanding as well as an assessment. You can also use task cards as a sponge activity and/or reinforcement of a skill that was previously taught.

Chapter Twenty Four

Diagramming

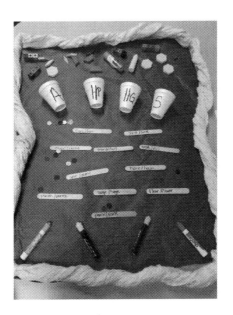

Methodology

Diagramming is done in many ways and for many reasons. I started to call this chapter break and sort because ultimately that is what it is. It is where you are allowing the student to break and sort different components of related material.

Directions

- Find the related material
- Make a cup or container of some sort into the smaller parts of the whole and then take the craft sticks and use it to print the items to sort and then allow the students to sort them and place them in the correct container.

I have used this for objectives such as;

- Parts of speech
- Homonym, synonyms, antonyms, homophones
- Sentence types
- Math facts
- Carnivores, herbivores, omnivores
- Odd and even numbers

Resources

For this activity I normally just use craft sticks and paper cups with some sort of weight in it so that the cups don't fall everywhere.

Educational Benefits

This allows for the student to visually discriminate closely related components. When done as a group, it allows for the opportunity to have a conversation that pertains to the objective and makes the student defend their choice.

Chapter Twenty Five

Intentional Grouping

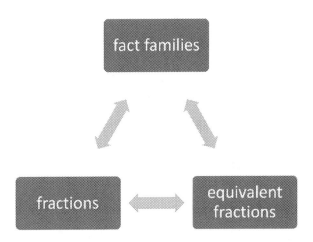

Methodology

Grouping is the magical component for every classroom but it can also be challenging at times. Intentional grouping is where you group students together on purpose to strengthen one or more skills at hand.

Directions

- Preassess a skill

- Go through the lesson cycle
- Posttest the skill
- Decide whether or not it is a skill that needs to be scaffold into mainstream instruction. If the answer is yes, I would group together the students who are having issues with the skill. In that same group I would also include a student teacher who can assist the students. I would also include a student that sort of has the skill just for the sake of debate and conversation.

Resources

Your data and simply knowledge of your students

Educational Benefits

The educational benefits of this methodology seems simple but many just don't get it or at least it seems that way. It takes a while to get to know your students. Once you get to know them and their personalities then you can use that to assist in the ways that you group them. The reason why this is called intentional grouping is because everything from the objective to the grouping is done by the teacher on purpose.

Chapter Twenty Six

Chart it/Either Or

Chart It				Either/Or			
Answer Choices	Question #			Answer Choices	Question #		
		1	2			1	2	3
	A				A			
	B				B			
	C				C			
	D				D			
% Correct				% Correct			

Methodology

In my other education book, the Data Driven Instructional Classroom I talk about the importance of data and the ability to desegregate data. Well here is a freebie of one way to collect data. This is actually two ways of gathering data in an informal way that you can use to see if a reteach or intervention is necessary in some form.

Directions

Chart It

With Chart it, you give the students a question with multiple choice answers. The students choose and answer and you have them to stand when you get to their answer choice. For Instance, you read the question aloud and you say, "Everyone who chose the letter A please stand." You count them and chart it next to the appropriate question number and answer choice. Then you say, "All of the ones who chose B please stand." You chart that one and so on. Then you work the problem and reveal the correct answer.

Either/Or

For Either/Or you pretty much do the same as you do for Chart It except you modify the answer choices down to only two choices instead of four and you ask the students is it either __or __ and allow them time to respond. You can also easily turn it into a debate and allow the students to defend their choices against each other.

I Say/You Say

With this game the teacher chooses an answer and proposes it to the class and then the class either agrees or disagrees and they must defend their answer, telling why the other choices are wrong or right.

Resources

For these activities all you really need is a dry erase marker and board and the sheets that you will be working with.

Educational Benefits

The educational benefits are endless for this activity. This activity allows the teacher to see if the message that she taught went over well or not by the number of questions that the students got correct. Also having the children defending their answer choice is the ultimate way of seeing if they attained the information that was taught successfully and it also forces them to critically think about what they are saying.

Conclusion

In no way is this an exhaustive list of interactive activities and I could have went on and on for chapters, and chapters but I had to stop somewhere. As I do in my classroom, I just want to get your engines turning and then turn you loose to be a victim to your own creativity. Being a teacher is all about passion and creativity and ever learning how to meet the demands of the current days. I will enclose a partial list of some of the resources that I use. Again please remember that I am in Texas and we are not a common core state so some of my resources may not apply to you but nothing says that you can't still use them and manipulate the resources to serve your purpose. Good luck and be creative as you create a new FUN environment for you and your students.

Index

Resources

Help for Reading Websites

Abcya- http://www.abcya.com/
IStation- http://www.istation.com/
Reading Eggs- https://app.readingeggs.com/login
Starfall- http://www.starfall.com/
Kids A-Z- https://www.kidsa-z.com/main/Login

Help for Math Websites

Think through Math- https://www.thinkthroughmath.com/
IXL- https://www.ixl.com/signin/
Reasoning Minds- https://my.reasoningmind.org/

Help for multiple subjects

Discovery Learning- http://www.discoveryeducation.com/
Study Island- http://www.studyisland.com/
Encyclopedia Britannica- http://school.eb.com/
Brain Pop- https://www.brainpop.com/
Imagine Learning- http://www.imaginelearning.com/
K-5 Learning- http://www.k5learning.com/

In no way is this a complete list of websites but just some of the most commonly used. Simply googling the grade and subject will give you a plethora of resources to use to assist your child.

Teacher Resources

Pinterest- https://www.pinterest.com/
Teachers Pay Teachers- https://www.teacherspayteachers.com/
K-5 Learning- http://www.k5learning.com/
Youtube- http://youtube.com

Help for Reading Websites

Abcya- http://www.abcya.com/
IStation- http://www.istation.com/
Reading Eggs- https://app.readingeggs.com/login
Starfall- http://www.starfall.com/
Kids A-Z- https://www.kidsa-z.com/main/Login

Help for Math Websites

Think through Math- https://www.thinkthroughmath.com/
IXL- https://www.ixl.com/signin/
Reasoning Minds- https://my.reasoningmind.org/

Help for multiple subjects

Discovery Learning- http://www.discoveryeducation.com/
Study Island- http://www.studyisland.com/
Encyclopedia Britannica- http://school.eb.com/
Brain Pop- https://www.brainpop.com/
Imagine Learning- http://www.imaginelearning.com/
K-5 Learning- http://www.k5learning.com/
*Common Core Sheets- http://www.commoncoresheets.com/

*Even though Texas is not a common core state, nothing says that we cannot use their resources. You just have to look for the objective as Texas is ahead of the common core standards.

There are also a number of websites that you can get from your school and/or district as well.

Dr. Jennifer Gilbert, ED.D.

Dr. Jennifer Gilbert is a seasoned teacher that has worked throughout the state of Texas and the surrounding areas. She has also worked overseas teaching English as a Second Language. She was born in Lawton, Oklahoma but raised worldwide by a military family but always knew that she wanted to be an educator.

She is an honored high school graduate of Bradwell Institute in Hinesville, Georgia, Class of 1993. She completed the beginning of her college career with a High Honored Associates in Child Development and Business Administration and has completed her Bachelors in the same areas of expertise at Tarleton State University. She also completed her masters in Adult Education and Training at the University of Phoenix. She has her Ph.D. in Christian Education from Northwestern Theological Seminary School and has completed all but her dissertation for her Educational Doctorates (Ed.D).

Dr. Gilbert has taught as the teacher of record for several grade levels from PRE-K through 5th grade in some of the largest districts in the state of Texas to include; Houston, Dallas, and Killeen and even some charter schools and served as substitute throughout her collegiate career for many other grades. Some other professional positions she has or has held is: Youth Pastor, Head of Youth Drama Ministry, Head of Youth Mime Ministry, Head of Christian Education, Pres. Of the YPD (young people's division), Director of Education for Sylvan Learning Center, Special Education Coordinator, part time teacher for Huntington Learning Center as well as the founder and CEO of her own educational consultation company JGM Educational Consultants.

Dr. Gilbert's greatest love, second to God, are her two children, Damaria and J'Donte (J.J.) Henderson who reside in Texas as the pursue their own collegiate careers and personal aspirations and her grandson Ethan J'Cean Henderson.

Her famous quote is, "Give me a mind and I will return a miracle." She believes that education is possible for all who desire it. No matter the labels that are placed on an individual. She came to this conclusion when her own biological son was diagnosed with medical obstacles but she reared him to believe that he can and will learn and despite the labels he graduated from High School on time and he lives a productive, independent life.

She is embarking upon her many works through her Christian books, "Churchin' Ain't Easy" released 2011 and "...And Deliver Us from People..." released in 2012, her book, "For the Perfecting of the Saints: The Five Biblical Ministry Gifts and What They Mean to You" released in 2014 and "365 Revelatory Words for any Given Day: A devotional" She also shares her passion through her educational books entitled, "The Data Driven Classroom Experience" due to release in 2017 along with many others. She has also released gospel cd single "Can I Just Be Me?", full length gospel cd entitled "Love Covers All" with business partner Cacean Ballou. She is also the owner and CEO of JGM Educational Consultants as well as the founder of Kingdom-Centered Life Changing Educational Conventions that seeks to assist in furthering the education and ensuring the educational success of students of all ages from Pre-K to Post Grads both secularly and in religion. To God be all the glory!

Printed in the United States
By Bookmasters